Judith Harries

Series editor
ALISTAIR
BRYCE-CLEGG

50

fantastic ideas for
caring for living things

FEATHERSTONE

FEATHERSTONE
Bloomsbury Publishing Plc
50 Bedford Square, London, WC1B 3DP, UK
29 Earlsfort Terrace, Dublin 2, Ireland

BLOOMSBURY, FEATHERSTONE and the Feather logo are trademarks of Bloomsbury Publishing Plc

First published in Great Britain, 2022 by Bloomsbury Publishing Plc
This edition published in Great Britain, 2022 by Bloomsbury Publishing Plc

A catalogue record for this book is available from the British Library

ISBN: PB: 978-1-8019-9047-9; ePDF: 978-1-8019-9048-6

2 4 6 8 10 9 7 5 3 1

Series design by Lynda Murray
Design by Jeni Child

Printed and bound in India by Replika Press Pvt. Ltd

MIX
Paper from
responsible sources
FSC® C016779

FSC
www.fsc.org

To find out more about our authors and books visit www.bloomsbury.com
and sign up for our newsletters

Contents

Introduction

Everything in the universe is connected and by helping children to understand this unity, they will gain a deeper awareness of themselves, others and all living things. Children learn in a holistic way and their understanding of the world is enhanced through learning in all areas of the Early Years curriculum. Learning through play is essential. Playing and enjoying nature will help children to learn how to care for living things.

As with all skills, caring for living things requires regular practice. Practising it will help children to develop empathy and compassion for each other and the world around them, and my hope is that the activities in this book will also help practitioners to build empathy alongside the children in their care. No specialist training is required, just an openness to gaining more understanding of the world through practical experiences of observing, caring for and respecting animals, insects, birds and plants.

Development Matters (Department for Education, 2020), states that children are expected to 'begin to understand the need to respect and care for the natural environment and all living things'. As well as building empathy, contact with natural surroundings is an important part of nurturing wellbeing among children and adults. There are many opportunities in this book for experiencing awe and wonder as the children find out about the animal kingdom, watch animals and plants grow, share and care for pets, observe a variety of lifecycles, build homes for different creatures, and find out how to help some endangered animals such as hedgehogs and bees.

As the RSPCA actively discourages the idea of keeping pets in settings, practitioners are advised instead to use visits, visitors, role play and books to bring some aspects of the natural world into the setting. Some activities encourage settings to explore natural habitats outside and even create habitats themselves so children can experience nature first-hand, see for example 'Wildflower garden', 'Hosting hedgehogs' and 'Minibeast manor'. There are some more long-term activities that involve waiting for something to grow, such as 'Beans means…' and 'Acorn to oak', or to be built, like the beetle home in 'Busy beetles', which require a fair amount of patience.

The late children's books author, Anna Dewdney, defined empathy as the 'understanding that other people have feelings, and those feelings count' (Dewdney, 2013). She believed that reading books with children helps them to see the world through someone else's eyes. While there may be some limitations to caring for living things in the nursery setting, a good book is often available, and many are recommended as part of these activities. Don't worry if you cannot get a copy as many are available online as read-aloud books.

The idea of caring for living things is extended further in the book through activities that encourage children to care about the current environmental crisis in which we find ourselves. In 'Oceans and rockpools' and 'Little collectors', for example, the children can get more involved in caring for the planet.

With thanks to my sister, Janice Bridger, an exceptional science teacher and nature lover.

Department for Education (2020), 'Development matters: Non-statutory curriculum guidance for the early years foundation stage', www.gov.uk/government/publications/development-matters--2

Dewdney, A. (2013), 'How Books Can Teach Your Child to Care', *The Wall Street Journal*, www.wsj.com/articles/BL-SEB-76229

Useful websites

Planning an outing or educational visit:
www.educationalvisitsuk.com
www.planmyschooltrip.co.uk

Contact an animal or wildlife welfare charity:
education.rspca.org.uk
www.wildlifetrusts.org.uk
butterflyconservation.org
www.hedgehogstreet.org
www.friendsoftheearth.uk
www.theowlstrust.org

Adopt an animal:
www.wwf.org.uk
www.bornfree.org.uk

Special occasions:
www.nationalpetmonth.org.uk
www.insectweek.co.uk
www.bigbutterflycount.org
rspb.org.uk

Resources for learning outside the classroom:
animalkind.org.uk
www.nationalgeographic.com
www.treetoolsforschools.org.uk
www.wildaboutgardens.org.uk
www.insectlore.co.uk
www.woodlandtrust.org.uk
www.worcswildlifetrust.co.uk
www.countryfile.com
www.forestschoolassociation.org

How to use this book

It is a good idea to read through each activity before you start in case you want to change the order, or just pick and choose one part to do. Anything is possible.

What you need lists the resources needed for each activity. These are likely to be readily available in most settings or can be bought or made easily.

What to do provides step-by-step instructions on how to carry out the activity. It often includes key information on the topic to help the practitioner feel more confident and to be more knowledgeable. Pick and choose the activity depending on the interests of the children in your setting, the resources and especially the time available.

Top tip gives a brief word of advice or helpful tip that could make all the difference to how you and the children experience the activity. It may include websites, books or optional resources that would enhance the activity.

What's in it for the children? details some of the benefits that the children will gain through the activities and how they will contribute to their learning. These are useful to share with staff, parents and carers and inspectors.

Taking it forward takes the activity to another level, often by suggesting games, creative activities, fiction and non-fiction books for further reading and input to extend the children's learning.

Health & Safety is only included if there are particular issues to be noted and addressed, above and beyond usual health and safety measures. Remember to always write a risk assessment for external trips and for activities involving visitors entering the setting.

Living and non-living things

Try some simple classification

What you need:

- A shoe box with a lid
- A selection of natural materials, such as a shell, a starfish, a feather, a sponge, a smooth pebble, a crystal and a stick
- A collection of objects or pictures to sort and classify, such as a dog, a hen, a fish, a tree, a flower, a stone, an ice cube, a button, a toothbrush, a cactus, a house, a car and a boat
- Two coloured hoops
- A camera

What to do:

1. Create a 'touch-and-feel box' by cutting a hole into the top of a shoe box; ensure that the hole is big enough for a child's hand to fit through. Add some natural materials to the box (see 'What you need').

2. Invite the children to touch the objects and ask them to tell you how things feel, for example smooth, rough or tickly. Take each item out and look at it carefully.

3. Talk about living and non-living things with the children. Can they tell you some things that are living? (Animals, plants and humans.)

4. Introduce some of the ways to recognise or categorise living things. For example, they need air to breathe, food to eat and water to drink. They can move (on their own), grow and reproduce.

5. Make a collection of different objects or pictures to sort and classify (see 'What you need').

6. Label two hoops 'living' and 'non-living' and ask the children to sort the objects into the correct hoops. Take photos of the two sets for you and the children to refer back to.

7. Can the children find some new things within the setting or from home to add to the sets?

Top tip ⭐

You could collect things on a scavenger hunt (see page 8) for the children to observe, sort and classify.

What's in it for the children?

This is a good way to introduce the topic of living things to the children and to help them to become aware of the wonderful diversity in the world around them.

Taking it forward

- Refine the activity to include three different classifications: living, no-longer living and never lived. What is the difference between a fallen leaf and a leaf growing on a tree? Or a piece of paper that used to be part of a living tree?

- Show the children a time-lapse film of a flower opening or a plant growing.

Scavenger hunt
Discovering treasures all around us

What you need:

- An outside area, garden, park, beach or woodland
- A list of things to find, using either pictures or words, such as leaf, flower, bird, butterfly, stone, feather, tree and cloud
- Treasure bags or boxes
- Paper cut into leaf shapes
- Sticky tape
- Magnifying glasses
- A muffin or cupcake tin

Top tip

Remind the children that if they are not sure if it is safe to pick something up, they should ask a grown-up.

What's in it for the children?

Children will explore the natural world around them and make close-up observations of plants and animals.

Taking it forward

- Go on a colour scavenger hunt using a sheet of paper containing a range of different colours. Ask the children to try to match each colour with found objects.

✚ Health & Safety

Make sure you take enough grown-ups with you on the scavenger hunt so that the children are safe and have plenty of support.

What to do:

1. Choose a suitable outside environment for children to access for the scavenger hunt.

2. Invite the children to use all their senses. Ask questions, such as 'What can you smell?', 'What can you hear?' and so on.

3. Provide the children with a list of things to find on the nature scavenger hunt (see 'What you need'). Vary the list according to the environment. Can they tick off the things they find on the list?

4. Ask the children to collect a few natural objects to look at more closely. Provide each child with a paper leaf and some sticky tape. Can they stick their finds onto the leaf? (This limits the number of natural objects they can select.) Encourage the children to use magnifying glasses to observe the objects in detail.

5. Sort through the treasures by labelling a muffin tray with leaf, flower, pebble, grass, and so on. Encourage the children to work with a partner to find items to put in the tray.

Night and day
Who comes out at night to play?

What you need:

- *Night Monkey, Day Monkey* by Julia Donaldson
- Pictures of nocturnal animals, such as bats, badgers, foxes, hedgehogs, owls and moths
- A feely bag with small items inside, such as a feather, a stone, a pine cone, a teaspoon, a comb, a tissue and a toothbrush
- Moth shapes cut out of coloured paper
- Paints and paintbrushes

What's in it for the children?

Children will understand the difference between night and day and will find out about nocturnal animals that are only active at night.

Taking it forward

- Introduce and talk to the children about our five senses.
- Encourage parents and carers to take their children outside into gardens at night or to sit in the bedroom in the dark. How does it feel? How much can they see? What can they hear? Are there any different smells?

What to do:

1. Talk about the concept of day and night. What do the children do at night? Discuss bedtime routines including bath time, stories and lullabies.

2. Read *Night Monkey, Day Monkey* to the children. Talk about the different things that the two monkeys see in each other's worlds.

3. Introduce nocturnal animals and insects that are active at night, such as bats, badgers, foxes, hedgehogs, owls and moths. Look at the pictures collected or at films online of these different animals.

4. Provide the children with a feely bag of small items for them to identify without looking, using just their senses of hearing and touch. How many items can they guess?

5. Discuss how nocturnal animals use different senses to survive in the dark. Owls have very good eyesight, hedgehogs use their sense of smell and bats use a special sonar system to find food and shelter.

6. Try some creative activities related to night and day. Night Monkey thinks the butterflies are 'Moths wearing make-up'. Let the children change some plain coloured moths into brightly decorated butterflies using the cut out moth shapes and paints.

Hibernating hints

Why do some animals sleep all winter?

What you need:

- A story about animals hibernating, such as *It Was a Cold, Dark Night* by Tim Hopgood or *Bear Snores On* by Karma Wilson
- A sand or tuff tray
- A selection of natural objects, such as pine cones, acorns and conkers
- Items to make a den, such as a tent, tunnels, blankets and cushions
- Hot chocolate (optional)

Top tip

Guide children who are interested in this topic to discover more information in helpful non-fiction books such as *Winter Sleep: A Hibernation Story* by Sean Taylor and Alex Morss.

What's in it for the children?

The children will become more aware of different animal behaviours and how they are affected by the environment in which they live.

Taking it forward

- Play a game of 'Sleeping Bear'. Sit in a circle and invite one child to sit in the middle and pretend to be a sleeping bear. The children can take turns to creep up to the bear and take away a pot of honey without waking him or her up.

What to do:

1. Introduce the idea of hibernation, whereby some animals sleep all through the winter and wake up in the spring. Animals that hibernate in the UK include hedgehogs, dormice, bats, and some species of insects such as bumblebees, butterflies, moths and ladybirds.

2. Ask the children why they think animals might hibernate. What do the children like to do when it is cold?

3. Read the children a story about an animal hibernating and ask questions such as, 'What do animals have to do before they hibernate?' and 'Where might they store their food?'.

4. Place some leaves in a sand or tuff tray and let the children hide acorns, pine cones or conkers for each other to find. How many can they spot?

5. Hold a 'hibernating party' and invite the children to come to the setting wearing pyjamas and dressing gowns. Build a dark den or cave using a tent, a tunnel, blankets and cushions for the children to sit on. Let them choose a bear or soft toy to take in the cave with them. Drink hot chocolate and read stories about hibernating animals.

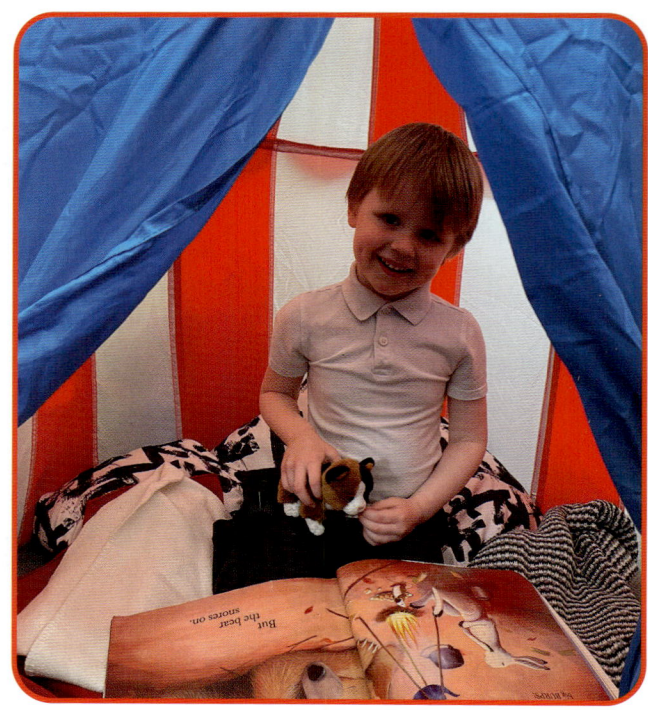

Clever camouflage
Animals playing hide and seek

What you need:

- A sand tray
- Green leaves
- Plastic toy frogs or frogs cut out from green paper
- Pictures of animals that use camouflage, such as butterflies, deer, fish, frogs, birds and tigers
- Small world animals or laminated pictures of animals
- Outline pictures of a butterfly, a moth, a bird and a fish
- Paper
- Colouring pencils, crayons or felt-tip pens

What's in it for the children?

Children will begin to understand how and why different animals use their appearance to help them to survive in nature.

Taking it forward

- Read *The Mixed-Up Chameleon* by Eric Carle who changes colour so he can blend in, but also to express his feelings. Ask the children which colour they feel like today and why.

What to do:

1. Play a game of hide and seek with the children to introduce the idea of camouflage. If they are wearing school uniform is the game harder?

2. Fill the sand tray with green leaves and then add some green toy or paper frogs for the children to take turns to find. Ask them how easy they are to spot.

3. Discuss the idea that some animals use camouflage to hide from other animals (predators) or to confuse their prey.

4. Look at pictures online or in non-fiction books of animals using different types of camouflage – blending in, changing shape, or using self-decoration and mimicry.

5. Why do the children think that polar bears are white? (To blend in with the Arctic landscape.) Why do some butterflies have spots on their wings? (So that they look like eyes and are off-putting to the birds that might want to eat them.)

6. Ask the children to choose an animal outline of a butterfly, moth, bird or fish and then colour it in so that it blends in with the surroundings. Let them choose where in the room their animal will be hiding and encourage them to try to match the colours.

Pet pie chart

A simple survey of pets

What you need:

- Pictures of different pets, such as a dog, a cat, a guinea pig and a fish
- Pictures of pie charts
- Coloured ribbons or string

Top tip

If children haven't got a pet at home, they could talk about a family or friend's pet.

What's in it for the children?

Children will be able to talk to the group confidently and share information about their own pets. They will learn how to record information in a pie chart.

Taking it forward

- Using the information from the pet pie chart, support the children to draw their own mini pet pie charts using paper plates and coloured pens.

- Start a display entitled 'Our Pets' and hang up the mini pie charts.

What to do:

1. Start off the topic of pets by showing the children a photo of your pet, or a family or friend's pet, and telling them all about him or her.

2. Talk about pets with the children. Which pets do the children have at home? What is their pet called? How do they help to take care of their pet?

3. Invite the children to sit in a circle so everybody can see and hear each other.

4. Explain that you are going to create a pet pie chart to record all the pets in the group. Show the children some pictures of pie charts.

5. Sort the children into groups around the circle so that all the children with dogs sit together, all the children with cats sit together, and so on. The children who don't have a pet could be called the 'not-yet-got-a-pet' group.

6. Attach the ribbons in the centre of the circle and stretch them out to divide the circle into slices for each different pet group.

7. Talk about what the pie chart tells us. Which is the most or least popular type of pet? Has anybody got an unusual or exotic pet such as a tarantula, bearded dragon, stick insect or snake?

I want a pet
Caring for pets at home

What you need:

- Funny stories about pets, such as *I Want a Pet* by Lauren Child, *What Pet Should I Get?* by Dr. Seuss, *Aaaarrgghh Spider!* by Lydia Monks or *The Pet* by Catherine Emmett
- A white board and pen
- A large papier mâché egg
- A soft toy bird or reptile

Top tip

To make a pretend egg, cover a balloon with several layers of papier mâché. Leave to dry and paint any colour you like; add some cracks to show it's ready to hatch.

What's in it for the children?

Children will become more aware of what they need to do to care for a pet including providing the basic needs of water, food and shelter.

Taking it forward

- Open a pet shop in the role-play corner. Provide lots of different types of pet food, bowls, cages, bedding and soft toy animals.

What to do:

1. Read the children a funny story about pets. Talk about why the children might want a particular pet. What do they think makes a good pet or companion animal?

2. Watch a film online about how to take care of a pet, such as a puppy, a rabbit or a fish.

3. Make a list with the children of what they might need to do to care for a pet in addition to providing food, water and shelter. Include exercise, groom, play with, keep safe, and of course, love.

4. Hide and then pretend to find a large papier mâché egg in the room. Let it hatch and break open over night to reveal a soft toy bird or reptile inside. Introduce the toy to the children as the class pet. Choose a name together.

5. Invite the children to take turns to look after the class pet and remind them to look at the list of needs you made together.

6. Take photographs of the children caring for the class pet to display during Pet Week (see page 16) and on an 'Our Pets' display.

✚ Health & Safety

Explain to the children that pet shops are not allowed to sell kittens and puppies, so it is safer to get a pet from a rescue centre run by the RSPCA or another animal charity.

Pet partnerships

Looking after a pet together

What you need:

- *We Honestly Can Look After Your Dog* by Lauren Child
- Soft and plastic toy animals
- Access to a role-play pet shop (see page 13)
- Blankets and cushions
- Picnic food (real or pretend)

What to do:

1. Explain to the children that they are going to use what they have already learned about pets to work with a partner and look after a pet for the day. They must try to keep the pet with them throughout the day and take care of all its needs.

2. Read *We Honestly Can Look After Your Dog* to the children or watch *Charlie and Lola: I Can Train Your Dog* or *I Completely Know About Guinea Pigs* online to show what could go wrong when looking after a pet.

3. Put the children into pairs and allocate each pair a soft toy or plastic toy animal. Try to have lots of different types of pets including some more exotic ones such as snakes, geckos, terrapins and tarantulas.

4. Encourage the children to visit the pet shop and buy supplies for their pets.

5. Set up a pet picnic area with blankets, cushions and picnic treats where pairs can gather together and share news about their pets. The children could share their snack as a picnic inside or outside.

What's in it for the children?

Children will be able to work together cooperatively and to gain an understanding of each other's feelings as they care for their pretend pets.

Taking it forward

- Set up a 'pet facts corner' for children to visit if they want to find out more or have any problems with their pet during the session.

- Provide the children with a selection of non-fiction books about pets to consult. Support them to look at some useful pet websites, such as young.rspca.org.uk; www.pdsa.org.uk; www.bluecross.org.uk and www.woodgreen.org.uk.

50 fantastic ideas for caring for living things

Pet week
Bring a pet to school

What you need:

- Invitations
- A calm, quiet area for animals
- Pets or photos of pets
- Sketching materials, such as paper, pencils and charcoal
- Easels
- Paints and paintbrushes

What's in it for the children?

This activity will allow children to have first-hand contact with a range of domestic animals and to develop their understanding of animal behaviour. They will also be able to make observations and create sketches and portraits.

Taking it forward

- Make a book about Pet Week including information about all the pets that visited, together with photographs, sketches and portraits created by the children.

✚ Health & Safety

Be sensitive to any children who may be nervous around some larger animals such as dogs. Check with parents and carers for any children who have allergies and ensure that a risk assessment is carried out prior to the visit.

What to do:

1. Send out invitations to parents and carers for a variety of different pets to visit the setting during Pet Week.

2. Talk to the children about how to behave when the animals are visiting – sitting quietly and keeping still so as not to alarm the visitors. Can they think of some questions that they would like to ask?

3. Invite the children to introduce their pets to the group and ask them and their adults to share more information about each pet.

4. Invite the children who cannot bring their live pet to the setting to bring a photograph instead.

5. Support the children to make sketches of the different animals using paper, pencils or charcoal.

6. Take photos of the different pets and their owners. Use the sketches and photos to help the children to paint portraits of the pets.

Top tip

This activity will require careful planning and it is best to only have one pet visiting at a time. You can use the information gleaned from the pet survey (see 'Pet pie chart' on page 12).

Fantasy pets
Make your own pet

What you need:

- Clay or salt dough
- A range of craft materials, such as matchsticks, pipe cleaners, feathers and googly eyes
- Clay tools
- Scissors
- Junk modelling materials, such as cardboard boxes, cardboard tubes, shredded paper and fabric
- Pebbles (optional)
- Acrylic paints in a range of colours (optional)
- Paintbrushes (optional)

What's in it for the children?

Children will use their imaginations, a variety of materials and expressive arts skills to create their own fantasy pet and share their creations.

Taking it forward

- Organise a pet show for the children to display and show off their newly created pets. Invite them to take turns to 'introduce' their pet to the group. Can they think of a name for their pet and talk about its needs?
- Present rosettes and awards for the best pet creations. Take photographs or display the models around an 'Our Pets' display.

✚ Health & Safety

Remind the children to take care when handling scissors and other tools.

What to do:

1. Explain to the children that they are going to create their own fantasy pets using lots of different modelling materials.

2. Start with a lump of clay or salt dough. Ask the children to mould a body shape and a head, and then add matchstick or pipe cleaner limbs. How many arms or legs will it have?

3. Can they make a face with googly eyes? Will their pet have ears or antennae?

4. Will their pet be able to fly? Try adding feathers to make wings.

5. Will their pet have scales? Try printing repeated scale patterns using clay tools.

6. Challenge the children to use recycled materials to make a bed, cage or hutch for the pets.

7. Alternatively, invite the children to make pebble pets by painting pebbles with acrylic paints. They could make stripy bees, creepy crawlies or tiny mice.

Top tip ⭐

Use this activity to help the children to imagine what it might feel like to have their own pet.

Pets at the vets

Open a role-play vet's surgery

What you need:

- Soft toy animals
- White coats or tabards
- A computer or keyboard
- Stethoscopes
- Weighing scales
- Bandages
- Pretend medicines
- Boxes or carriers for pets

What's in it for the children?

An important part of caring for a pet is looking after it when it gets ill and through this activity children will develop an understanding of the role of a vet.

Taking it forward

- Teach the children a song about a poorly pet:

  I have got a poorly pet,

  Poorly pet, poorly pet.

  He/she needs to see the vet

  To mend his/her poorly paw/leg/ tail/nose.

  Sing it to the tune of 'Mary Had a Little Lamb' as you pass a toy pet around the circle. The child holding the pet on the last word of the song has to choose where it hurts.

What to do:

1. Research information about caring for sick, injured and homeless pets at www.bluecross.org.uk. The charity offers free talks to Early Years settings about caring for pets.

2. Talk about taking pets to the vet and relate it to the doctor who we visit when feeling poorly. Explain to the children that vets often have to give vaccinations, prescribe anti-flea and worm medications or help animals in emergencies. They help us to look after animals and keep them safe, healthy and happy.

3. Set up a vet surgery in the role-play corner with lots of medical equipment, an examination table, computer and weighing scales.

4. Encourage the children to take turns to role play as the vet, nurse or the owner with a pet. Encourage the children to think about how the owners might be feeling if their pet is poorly.

5. Support the children to weigh pets, measure out medicines, give injections and put bandages on injured limbs.

Farmyard fun

I went to visit a farm one day

What you need:

- A local rural or city farm to visit
- Fiction and non-fiction books about farm animals
- Pictures of farm animals
- Paper
- Pencils and crayons

What's in it for the children?

Children will be introduced to different farm animals and crops through visits, books and games. They will compare similarities and differences between the animals.

Taking it forward

- Play a game of 'Farmyard Fun' based on 'Beans'. Invite the children to move like a horse, trotting or galloping. Add a neighing sound. Ask the children to change to a duck, quacking, gliding on the water or waddling along, or a sheep, baaing, walking slowly on all fours and stopping to eat some grass. Gradually add different animals and encourage the children to invent their own moves as you shout out the animals. How will the pigs or chickens move about?

What to do:

1. Before the farm visit, talk about what animals the children expect to see. What else do farmers look after on farms? Show the children pictures of different farm animals and crops. Read stories and look at non-fiction books about farms.

2. After the visit learn the song 'I Went to Visit a Farm One Day'. Make a list of the different animals or plants the children saw at the farm.

3. Play a guessing game with the children. Say three or four sentences about a farm animal, such as 'I have four legs. I eat grass. I say moo!' or 'I have a curly tail. I like rolling in mud. I say oink!' Can the children identify each mystery animal?

4. Make a mystery 'Who am I?' book with the children. Support the children to write short sentences on one page and draw a picture or add a photo of the farm animal on the next page. Use photos from the farm trip or drawings made by the children.

✚ Health & Safety

Ensure that a risk assessment is carried out before the visit. If the children come in close contact with animals remind them to wash their hands.

Old MacDonald

Design your own farm

What you need:

- *Farmer Duck* by Martin Waddell and Helen Oxenbury
- Small world farm animals
- A large sheet of paper
- A map or plan of a farm
- Farm buildings
- Paper and pencils

Top tip

Set up a small world farm for the children to experience playing with before challenging them to design their own.

What's in it for the children?

Children find out about the varied work of a farmer and learn about basic farming.

Taking it forward

- Divide the children into groups and ask each group to create a farm collage board. They could use corrugated cardboard for ploughed fields, shiny blue paper for a pond and different fabric for unploughed fields.
- Open a farmer's market in the role-play area. Provide lots of pretend or real fresh fruit and vegetables for the children to sell.

What to do:

1. Read *Farmer Duck* to the children. Talk to them about all the work Farmer Duck had to do while the farmer lay in his bed. Make a list with the children of the different jobs the farmer has to do on the farm.

2. Encourage lots of imaginative play with the small world farm animals.

3. Explain to the children that they are all going to be farmers and design their own farm. Sing 'Old MacDonald' and let the children substitute their names in the song.

4. Brainstorm on a large piece of paper all the different animals, crops and buildings that they could include. Show the children a simple plan or map of a farm that they could follow.

5. Support the children to draw a picture or plan showing the layout of their own farm. Where will they put the cows or the sheep? Are they going to grow any vegetables? Do they need a barn, a stable, a pigsty and a farmhouse to live in?

6. Help the children to add labels to their plan for the different animals and buildings. Support younger children with their writing by providing a list of animal names for them to copy.

Charming chickens
Finding out about caring for chickens

What you need:

- A visitor to talk about chickens or a workshop run by the British Hen Welfare Trust (BHWT)
- Non-fiction books about chickens
- Photographs of chickens
- Four large pieces of card
- Felt-tip pens

Top tip

To find out more about rehoming chickens in your setting, or to sponsor a chicken, visit the British Hen Welfare Trust at www.bhwt.org.uk.

What to do:

1. Invite a visitor who keeps chickens to come into the setting to talk to the children, or arrange a BHWT workshop so that the children can interact with chickens whilst learning how to care for them.

2. What do the children already know about chickens? Invite the children to prepare questions beforehand to ask the visitor.

3. Talk about the different features of a chicken – beak, wattle, comb, feathers, scaly legs, tail and so on.

4. Introduce the idea of the life cycle: egg – chick – hen – egg. Encourage the children to draw or paint pictures of the chickens, chicks and eggs. Display their artwork as a life cycle.

5. Play a game of 'Who am I like?'. Write short sentences that describe a chicken on four pieces of card, such as 'I have wings', 'I have a beak' and 'I lay eggs'. Place them in the four corners of the room. Shout out the names of different animals and ask the children to run to the corner of the room that has the card with a matching characteristic.

What's in it for the children?

Children will observe chickens and find out more about how to care for them. They will be able to make the connection between chickens and the tasty eggs that they eat.

Taking it forward

- Share some egg sandwiches or boiled eggs and soldiers at snack time.

Health & Safety

Carry out a risk assessment prior to the visit and make sure the children wash their hands thoroughly after coming into contact with the chickens.

Hide and sheep

How do sheep help us?

What you need:

- Pictures of sheep
- Non-fiction books about sheep
- Toy plastic sheep and lambs
- Real sheep wool
- Balls of wool in a range of different colours
- Paper plates
- A hole punch
- Strips of ribbon and fabric

What to do:

1. Talk about sheep with the children and find out what they already know. Introduce the family – ewe, ram and lamb. Look at pictures, watch films online and read non-fiction books about sheep.

2. Share the nursery rhyme 'Little Bo Peep' with the children.

3. Play a game of 'Hide and Sheep'. Hide some toy sheep around your setting for the children to find.

4. Explain that farmers look after sheep because they provide us with wool, meat and dairy. In the spring, sheep don't need their warm woolly coats so the farmers shear them, rather like us having a haircut. We can use the wool to make clothes to keep us warm.

5. Sing 'Baa, Baa Black Sheep'. Show the children some real sheep wool and let them try pulling and twisting it into long pieces of yarn. Compare it with the balls of wool that are ready to use for knitting and weaving.

6. Support the children to try some weaving using a paper plate frame. Thread lengths of wool across the circle and tape or knot in place. Weave strips of ribbon and fabric in and out of the wool.

What's in it for the children?

Children will find out about how farmers care for sheep and how we use their wool to make clothes and insulate things.

Taking it forward

- Read *Charlie Needs a Cloak* by Tomie dePaola, a story about a young shepherd who shears his sheep, washes the wool, cards (separates and straightens) and spins it into yarn to weave into fabric.

- Investigate how wool can be used to insulate things by comparing what happens to two warm drinks: one with sheep wool wrapped around it and one without.

Top tip ⭐

Prepare the paper plates by cutting a circle out of the middle and punching holes around the ring.

Animal babies

Discovering animals and their young

What you need:

- Non-fiction books about baby animals, such as *Animal Babies* by Laura Barwick and *Discovery: Baby Farm Animals* by Thea Feldman
- Different-coloured plastic eggs
- Small world animals and their young, such as pig/piglet, cow/calf, sheep/lamb and horse/foal
- Word and picture cards of animals and their young

What's in it for the children?

Alongside learning lots of new vocabulary about animals and their young, children will be challenged to handle the eggs, opening and closing them in order to play the game, which will develop their fine-motor skills.

Taking it forward

- Extend the activity by including the names of male and female animals such as bull/cow, ram/ewe, stallion/mare and so on.
- Share *Monkey Puzzle* by Julia Donaldson with the children and talk about wild animals and their young.

What to do:

1. Start the activity by talking about the names of different animals and their babies that the children may already be familiar with. Some children may have experienced looking after a puppy or kitten at home.

2. Share some books about baby animals that have sounds. Talk with the children about what they think all the baby animals need from their parents. (Food, shelter and to be taught how to look after themselves in order to survive.)

3. Ask the children to sit in a circle. Place the adult and baby animals inside the plastic eggs and explain that the children are going to play 'Where's my mummy?'.

4. Place the eggs in the middle of the circle and invite the children to take turns to choose two eggs, open them up and see if the animals are a pair. If they are not, close the eggs and replace them in the middle of the group.

5. When all of the mummies are found and reunited with their babies, label them with word and picture cards.

Top tip ⭐

The 'Where's my mummy?' game works best with a small group of children. If the animals don't fit inside the eggs, cover with a plastic cup or bowl.

Cows in the kitchen

How do cows help us?

What you need:

- Pictures of cows
- Non-fiction books about cows
- A rubber or plastic glove
- Water
- A pin
- A bucket
- Milk
- Fresh fruit, such as bananas, strawberries and raspberries
- A hand-blender

What to do:

1. Talk about cows with the children and find out what they already know. Introduce the family – cow, bull and calf. Look at pictures, watch films online and read non-fiction books about cows with the children. Find out about different types of cattle such as Highland, Jersey and Friesian (black and white).

2. Explain that farmers look after cows that provide us with milk and meat. Cows are vegetarian so they only eat grass to make milk. Farmers milk the cows in the dairy and send the milk to supermarkets to be bought by us in cartons and bottles.

3. Fill a rubber or plastic glove with water and pierce a tiny hole in the end of one finger with a pin. Explain to the children that the glove acts like the cow's udder. Show the children how milk is extracted from the udder by letting them take turns to squeeze the water out of the glove into a bucket.

4. Make some different flavoured milk shakes with the children to share at snack time to celebrate how cows help us.

What's in it for the children?

Children will begin to understand that we care for cows and they provide us with different products.

Taking it forward

- Read *Cows in the Kitchen* by Airlie Anderson. Sing the song 'Cows in the Kitchen' to the tune of 'Skip to my Loo'.

    Cows in the kitchen, moo, moo, moo.

    Cows in the kitchen, moo, moo, moo.

    Cows in the kitchen, moo, moo, moo.

    What shall we do Tom Farmer?

- Find out about other animals that produce milk such as goats and sheep.

➕ **Health & Safety**

Make sure you are aware of any dairy allergies and other dietary requirements of the children.

Horsepower
Horses helping us to work

What you need:

- Large socks
- Bubble wrap or old tights
- Fabric pre-cut into triangles
- Wool made into plaits
- Buttons
- A needle and thread
- Long cardboard tubes, recycled broom or mop handles or wooden dowelling
- String
- Scissors
- Ribbon

What's in it for the children?

Children will discover how important horses are in the world and find out more about how to care for them.

Taking it forward

- The children can make mini hobby horses to take home using baby socks and old pencils.
- Open a role-play stable with stalls for the horses, lots of shredded paper for hay, name plaques for each horse and helpful signs telling children how to care for the horses.

What to do:

1. Talk to the children about how important horses have been to us in the past, before cars, tractors and trains. They worked on farms pulling ploughs, pulled carriages around towns and carried their riders across the country. Now they are mainly ridden for pleasure or sport.

2. Invite the children to share any experiences they have had with horses. Make a list with the children of ideas for how to care for them, such as feeding, providing shelter, grooming, exercising and so on.

3. Explain to the children that they are going to help make some hobby horses to look after and pretend to ride.

4. Ask the children to stuff a large sock with bubble wrap or old tights to make the horse's head. Attach plaits of wool as manes, triangles of fabric for ears and buttons for eyes using a needle and thread.

5. Post a long cardboard tube, length of wooden dowelling or old broom or mop handle up the neck of the stuffed head and secure with string. You can make a notch in the stick to tie the string around which makes the head more secure.

6. Make a halter and reins out of ribbon or strips of fabric.

7. Invite the children to think of names for the horses. Let them take turns riding the hobby horses.

Training dogs
How do dogs help us?

What you need:

- A large indoor or outdoor space suitable for an obstacle course
- Climbing equipment, such as steps, a ladder, a slide and balance beams
- Hoops
- Cones
- Tunnels
- Blindfolds
- Benches or mats
- Cardboard signs in different colours

What's in it for the children?

Children will be challenged to use their senses and to be aware of space at the same time as beginning to appreciate the clever work that trained dogs do.

Taking it forward

- Share some picture books about sheepdogs, such as *The Very Best Sheepdog* by Pinny Grylls and *Floss* by Kim Lewis.

 Health & Safety

Remind the children to take extra care on the obstacle course, especially when wearing blindfolds.

What to do:

1. Talk to the children about how dogs are often trained to do special jobs to help us. Some dogs are trained to help people who are blind or partially sighted, who are deaf, or who need help in other ways.

2. Set up an obstacle course for the children to explore using the equipment that you have available.

3. Invite the children to try out the course for themselves. Incorporate any suggestions they make to improve it.

4. Challenge the children to work with a partner and guide them around the obstacle course while they are wearing a blindfold. Discuss how guide dogs will protect their owners from danger.

5. Some dogs are trained to herd sheep and work on farms. Play a game of 'Rounding up the Sheep'. Set up four sheep stations in the room or outdoor space using benches or mats. Label each station with a coloured sign. Choose two children to be 'sheepdogs' and challenge them to sort the other children into the pens according to the colours they are wearing. Encourage the rest of the children to behave like sheep and go in the wrong direction!

Animal encounters

Getting up close with wildlife

What you need:

- A visit from a local animal expert
- A camera

Top tip

Either seek a personal recommendation for an animal workshop visit for the children or check out online reviews.

What's in it for the children?

Children will have opportunities to observe close up and even touch some more unusual animals and develop their understanding of the animal kingdom.

Taking it forward

- Learn some vocabulary for classifying wild animals, such as mammals, amphibians, birds, reptiles, fish and insects. Support the children to sort plastic animals and pictures into the different groups.

✚ Health & Safety

Carry out a risk assessment before the visit and check with parents and carers for any children who have allergies. Be sensitive to any children who may be nervous around live animals.

What to do:

1. Contact a local animal expert who can visit your setting and provide the children with a hands-on animal experience. You can sometimes choose the animals the expert will bring, which can often be fairly exotic, such as snakes, owls, tarantulas, bearded dragons, cockroaches and tortoises.

2. Talk to the children about how to behave when the animals are visiting – they should sit quietly and sit still, so they don't scare the animals.

3. Prepare some questions to ask the animal expert about how they care for the different animals. Talk to the children about the sorts of questions they would like to ask so that they are prepared. Encourage spontaneous questions too.

4. During the visit, ask the children how it feels to be close up to the amazing creatures. Are they surprised about how it feels when they stroke the snake's skin or the owl's feathers?

5. Take lots of photos and film the visit so the children can look back and remember the experience.

6. Go to animalkind.org.uk and watch 'Animal Kind Film', presented by Michela Strachan. This is also a good alternative if a visit is not possible.

Dear zoo

Adopt a wild animal

What you need:

- A range of non-fiction animal books
- *Dear Zoo* by Rod Campbell
- Paper
- Pencils
- Envelopes
- Stamps

Top tip ⭐

If you are near a zoo or safari park, organise a trip. Download a free set of animal cards from animalkind.org.uk for the children to use in their play.

What's in it for the children?

Children will find out more about how zoos work and consider the benefits and drawbacks. They will learn about adopting animals and how this helps to fund protection and conservation.

Taking it forward

- Share *Zoo* by Anthony Browne with the children. How do the children think the animals in the zoo are feeling? Why is the tiger pacing up and down? Discuss the pros and cons of zoos.

What to do:

1. Talk to the children about any visits that they have made to a zoo or safari park with their families. Which animals have they seen there? Explore with the children how zoos work hard to help endangered animals.

2. Make a list of some of the children's favourite animals. Look at books and pictures to illustrate the activity.

3. Share *Dear Zoo* with the children. The book starts with this opening sentence: 'I wrote to the zoo to send me a pet'. Ask the children why they think that none of the zoo animals is suitable as a pet.

4. Explain that adopting an animal is a good way to help protect endangered animals and invite the children to write letters to a local zoo asking to adopt one of the animals. Model the activity so that the children know the sorts of details to include, for example, they could ask for photos and information on a favourite animal.

5. Alternatively, go to one of these websites and adopt an animal on behalf of the children:

   • www.wwf.org.uk or www.bornfree.org.uk – adopt an animal such as an elephant, a penguin, a snow leopard, an orang-utan or a dolphin.

   • www.wildlifetrusts.org.uk – protect UK wildlife by adopting an animal such as a hedgehog, an otter, a red squirrel, an owl or a beaver.

Animal moves

Moving like lots of different creatures

What you need:

- A large indoor or outdoor space

Top tip

Read *I do it like this!* by Susie Brooks with the children. Compare how the children move, sleep, eat, wash and dance with how different animals carry out these activities.

What to do:

1. Talk to the children about the different ways we can move. Make a list, such as walking, hopping, jumping, marching, stretching, crawling, swimming and so on.

2. Watch 'How do Animals Move?' at tigtagjunior.com.

3. Make a list with the children of the ways in which animals move, such as flying and gliding, jumping, climbing trees, burrowing underground, swimming underwater, swinging from trees and running on all fours.

4. Support the children to compare the ways that humans move with three of the main ways that animals move: walking, swimming and flying.

5. Play a game based on 'Beans' where the children move like different creatures. Start with two contrasting moves and shout out the names of the animals, for example, 'cheetah' (run very fast) or 'butterfly' (flutter around with outstretched arms).

6. Gradually add more animals and more movements. Let the children use some of their own ideas. Try some of these: elephant (stomp around noisily), cat (stretch and pounce), tortoise (plod along slowly), snake (slither along on your tummy), fish (flap your arms like fins), kangaroo (jump on two legs), duck (waddle and wiggle your bottom) and monkey (stretch your arms up high and pretend to swing).

50 fantastic ideas for caring for living things

What's in it for the children?

Children will develop spatial awareness, will learn different ways to move around and will be able to practise coordinating their gross motor skills.

Taking it forward

- Try some movements in pairs. Can the children find a partner and crawl along like an eight-legged spider? Or make a line of four or five, holding arms around waists, and walking along together like a caterpillar?

- Add some music to the movement game. Use 'Carnival of the Animals' by Saint-Saëns or 'Mother Goose Suite' by Ravel.

 Health & Safety

Remind the children to take care not to bump into each other when moving around.

Animal patterns
Design a new coat for an animal

What you need:

- Pictures of wild animals with interesting coats
- Outlines of a range of animals, birds, reptiles and fish
- Scissors
- Glue
- Paints and paintbrushes
- A range of craft materials, such as coloured paper, textured fabrics, faux fur, shiny paper, buttons, sequins and feathers

What to do:

1. Look at pictures with the children of wild animals with different patterned coats. Make a list, such as tiger, zebra, leopard, jaguar, giraffe, ring-tailed lemur and so on.

2. Compare these furry animals with the patterns found on snakes, reptiles, fish and birds. Ask the children to choose their favourite coats.

3. Talk to the children about how animals use patterns to camouflage and hide from predators or prey (see 'Clever camouflage' on page 11) and how coats also keep animals warm or protect them from their environment.

4. Discuss with the children the way that some animals and insects use their stripes to warn other animals and insects that they are dangerous, for example wasps, while other animals and insects only pretend to be dangerous, such as hover flies.

5. Explain to the children that they are going to design some new animal coats using paints and craft materials. They can choose to 'coat' a furry animal, snake, fish or bird. Start with an outline of the chosen animal and then paint or cut and stick the new design together.

What's in it for the children?

Children will be able to recognise different patterned animal coats and to talk about their purpose. They will develop their artistic skills by designing a new pattern or coat.

Taking it forward

- Read *Greedy Zebra* by Mwenye Hadithi with the children, a traditional African folktale about how animals found their unique prints and colours.

 Health & Safety

Remind the children to take care when handling scissors and other craft tools.

Minibeast hunt

We're going on a minibeast hunt

What you need:

- Pictures of insects
- A wood, garden or local park
- Magnifying glasses
- Magnifying bug pots
- Pencils

Top tip

Change the words of 'We're going on a bear hunt' to 'We're going on a minibeast hunt' and sing with the children.

What's in it for the children?

Children will be encouraged to closely observe insects in their habitats and to compare similarities and differences.

Taking it forward

- Try using a smartphone app such as Picture Insect to identify any unusual insects or use the WWF Seek app to identify any living things.
- Find out about Insect Week, organised by the Royal Entomological Society, at www.insectweek.co.uk.

Health & Safety

Remind the children not to touch any insects that might sting or harm them and to wash their hands after completing the activity.

What to do:

1. Explain to the children that they are going to become entomologists (insect experts) and go on a hunt to look for minibeasts.

2. Look at pictures of different insects with the children and learn some vocabulary before you go outside, such as ladybird, bee, spider, ant, woodlouse, snail, caterpillar, butterfly, worm, fly, centipede and so on.

3. Go to www.treetoolsforschools.org.uk and download a free minibeast or creepy crawly spotter sheet to show the children pictures of what they might find. Use this as a resource during the hunt for children to annotate.

4. Choose an area outside where the children can 'grub about' amongst grass, leaves and soil to find different insects.

5. Ask the children to be very careful as they turn over stones and logs, look on the underside of leaves, and search in secret places for different insects. Remind the children to always put back anything they move during the hunt.

6. Use magnifying glasses and pots to observe insects more closely. Pop soil or leaf mould into the pot along with the minibeasts to make them feel at home.

Busy beetles

Build a beetle bucket

What you need:

- Fiction and non-fiction books about beetles
- A large exercise ball
- An outdoor space suitable for a beetle home
- A plastic bucket
- A craft knife
- A spade
- Stones
- Small logs
- Leaves

What's in it for the children?

Children can create a suitable habitat for beetles in the garden or outside area. They will begin to learn about the amazing diversity of creatures in the world.

Taking it forward

- Invite the children to design a beetle and draw or paint a picture. Remember that every beetle has one head, two antennae, one body, two sets of wings and six legs.

Health & Safety

Remind the children to wash their hands after handling leaves and soil.

What to do:

1. Look at some pictures of different beetles online and in books with the children. Enjoy learning some beetle names together, such as stag, dung and rhinoceros.

2. Watch a clip online of a dung beetle moving a huge ball of dung to turn it into their new home. Invite the children to be beetles pushing a large exercise ball around on all fours.

3. Explain that you are going to build a beetle bucket. Let children watch as you cut some 3 cm holes into the bottom and sides of a bucket so beetles can get in and out.

4. Take a small group of children outside and dig a hole deep enough to place the bucket inside.

5. Support the children to place a layer of stones at the bottom of the bucket and then to stand some logs upright on top of them.

6. Encourage the children to fill the bucket with leaves. Add a layer of soil on top and finally place another log on top to attract the beetles.

7. Invite the children to visit the beetle bucket after a week and look for beetles around it.

Butterfly ball
Discovering the life cycle of the butterfly

What you need:

- *The Very Hungry Caterpillar* by Eric Carle or *Cora Caterpillar* by Emma Tranter
- White paper
- Paints and paintbrushes
- Scissors

Top tip ⭐

Buy a butterfly garden kit for use in the setting so that the children can experience the life cycle first-hand.

What's in it for the children?

Children will learn about the life cycle of the butterfly and find out ways to help conserve butterflies and their habitats.

Taking it forward

- Some butterflies and moths are endangered. Go to butterfly-conservation.org and share with the children ways to help butterflies.

➕ Health & Safety

Remind the children to take care when handling scissors.

What to do:

1. Read about the caterpillar, pupa and butterfly in *The Very Hungry Caterpillar* or *Cora Caterpillar*. Talk about the life cycle of a butterfly or moth with the children. There are four stages and at each one they go through a metamorphosis (a complete change or transformation). Ask the children to draw a life cycle picture like this:

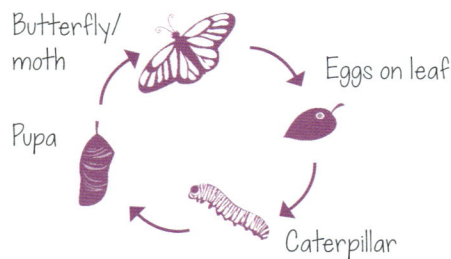

2. Explain to the children that moths are often smaller than butterflies, fold their wings differently and usually come out at night.

3. Invite the children to design their own butterfly or moth artwork. Talk about symmetry and how the wings must be identical.

4. Fold a piece of paper in half and then open it. Show the children how to paint a pattern using blobs of paint on one side, then fold the paper again and press. Are the wings symmetrical? When dry, support the children to cut the paper into the shape of wings and hang them up to display.

Stripy snails

Survey some snails and try a snail race

What you need:

- An outside space
- Snails
- A camera
- Nail varnish or white correction fluid
- A sheet of clear plastic
- A small carton of fruit juice

Top tip ⭐

This activity works best in the spring and summer when the weather is warm.

What's in it for the children?

This activity is a simple introduction to behaviour variation, adaptation and distribution of snails by observing them in the garden.

Taking it forward

- Encourage the children to look closely at the snails or photos and talk to them about the different parts of the snail – head, body, foot, shell and four tentacles (the top two are for seeing, the bottom two are for smelling).

✚ Health & Safety

Remind the children to wash their hands after touching snails or soil.

What to do:

1. Explain to the children that snails are often just regarded as garden pests, but actually they are clever cleaners and provide an important source of food for birds.

2. Ask the children to go outside and look for some snail trails to see if they can find any snails. Take photos so you can compare the snails.

3. Talk about the different colours of the shells and look to see if there are no bands (stripes), one band or many bands.

4. Help the children to place a tiny spot of nail varnish or paint on each shell as a marker. Explain to the children that by doing this they will be able to find out how far the snails move or if they come back to the same place every day. Have they got a homing instinct?

5. Let the children take part in some snail races. Place some snails in a line at one end of a plastic sheet. Drip a thin line of fruit juice in front of each snail to encourage them to move. Which snail moves fastest and wins the race?

Wily worms

Watching worms at work in a wormery

What you need:

- *Superworm* by Julia Donaldson
- A patch of ground
- Earthworms
- A 2 L clear plastic bottle
- Materials for filling the wormery, such as soil, compost, sand, scrap paper and fruit and vegetable peelings
- Leaves
- Water
- Scissors
- Cling film
- Elastic bands
- Black paper
- Sticky tape

What to do:

1. Explain to the children that worms play an important role in recycling and making the soil healthy. They also provide food for birds. Read *Superworm* by Julia Donaldson or watch the BBC animated film.

2. Cut the top off a plastic bottle and help the children to fill it with layers of soil, compost, sand, moist scrap paper and fruit and vegetable peelings. Show them how to carefully add a few worms to each layer.

3. Encourage the children to add fallen leaves on the top and to water until damp.

4. Place a piece of cling film over the top of the bottle and secure with an elastic band. Pierce a few holes in the cling film so that the worms can breathe.

5. Wrap black paper around the bottle and secure with sticky tape.

6. Leave the worms to work, but encourage the children to check the wormery regularly so that water can be added if the layers are drying out.

7. After a couple of weeks, remove the black paper so that the children can see if the worms have been busy. Have the layers been mixed together?

What's in it for the children?

Children can find out how worms work hard to aerate the soil. They will have hands-on experience of caring for worms and creating a suitable habitat.

Taking it forward

- Invite the children to try some 'worm charming' by dancing and stamping on the soil to create vibrations that attract worms. Add a worm chant such as:
  Worms, worms,
  charming worms,
  come and say hello!
  When it rains, when it pours,
  do not hide below!

Health & Safety

Remind the children to wash their hands after handling soil or worms.

Web designers

Admiring the wonderful world of spiders

What you need:

- Pictures of spiders and spider webs
- Chalks or masking tape

Top tip

If you or any of the children are scared of spiders try reading *I'm Just Not Keen on Spiders* by Lauren Child. Try not to let the children catch your fears!

What to do:

1. Explain to the children that it's easy to spot spider webs covered in morning dew on autumn mornings, but because spiders usually spin their webs at night, they can be difficult to find.

2. Take the children on a spider spotting expedition outside your setting. Explain to the children that spiders are good at catching flies and other insects in their webs. What do the children think cobwebs are?

3. Look on window frames and car wing mirrors, and search along fences, gates and walls. How many different places can they find webs? The spiders are even more difficult to spot!

4. Play I-spy spider with the children, whilst on the expedition:

   I spy, with my little eye,

   A spider on the …

5. When back at the setting, draw a giant spider web on the playground outside using chalk or inside using masking tape.

6. Play a game of 'Spider, Spider, Catch Me if You Can!'. Choose one child to be the spider waiting on the web. Invite another child to walk across the web trying not to tread on it. If they do touch the web, the spider is allowed to catch the 'fly' and they become the new spider.

✚ Health & Safety

Carry out a risk assessment before taking the children on the spider spotting expedition.

What's in it for the children?

Children can explore the natural world around them as they try to spot spiders. They will become aware of the change of the seasons.

Taking it forward

- Investigate with the children and find out about some different types of spiders at dkfindout.com.

- Make spider webs with the children. Mix some silver paint into a bottle of PVA glue. Support the children to dribble the glue onto a round plastic lid in the shape of a web. Once dry, peel the webs off the plastic and hang them in the windows.

Minibeast manor

Build a home for the minibeasts in your outdoor space

What you need:

- A suitable outdoor space
- Three or four wooden pallets
- Bricks (with holes in)
- A variety of materials to fill the gaps, such as sticks and twigs, straw, moss, leaves, bark, pinecones, sand, soil, corrugated cardboard, plastic bottles, toilet rolls, bamboo canes and stones
- Clay piping (optional)
- Tiles (optional)
- Terracotta flowerpots (optional)

What's in it for the children?

Children are involved in creating a special habitat to encourage lots of different creatures to thrive. They will also have the opportunity to observe the minibeasts' behaviour.

Taking it forward

- In the spring add a 'green growing roof' to the manor. Place material with drainage holes on top of the pallets. Fill the holes with compost and water. The children can rake the soil and sprinkle grass or chamomile seeds on top. Keep it watered and wait for the seeds to sprout.

Health & Safety

Carry out a risk assessment before starting the activity and make sure the children are carefully supervised during the building to avoid accidents.

What to do:

1. Talk to the children about how important minibeasts are to us for pollinating crops and keeping soil healthy. Explain that you are going to create a special habitat in the garden to help them thrive.

2. Choose a suitable quiet spot with flat, solid ground to build the minibeast manor.

3. Start with a base of bricks, placed slightly apart in an H shape. Stack the wooden pallets on top.

4. Ask the children to fill the gaps with the different materials that have been collected. Help them to create lots of different nooks and crannies, tunnels and cosy beds for the minibeasts to hide inside. Use dead wood and bark to encourage beetles, spiders and woodlice to move in.

5. Create small holes and use tubes to entice solitary bees and make bigger holes with stones and clay piping to attract toads. Fill flowerpots with leaves for earwigs to shelter inside.

6. Choose a regular time to take the children to observe the occupants of minibeast manor, encouraging them to use magnifying glasses for closer inspection. How many insects can they identify and name?

Frogs and toads
Find out about friendly amphibians

What you need:

- Bubble wrap
- Felt-tip pens
- Fingerpaints
- Green paper

Top tip ⭐

Watch the video 'Life Cycle of a Frog', by Peekaboo Kidz, or read *Franklin Frog* by Emma Tranter.

What's in it for the children?

Children can make observations of the life cycle of a frog and other amphibians and demonstrate their learning using mixed media.

Taking it forward

- Create a mini-pond in your garden using a washing up bowl or old sink. For more help on creating a pond, watch 'Gardening with Children: Dawn and Archie Build a Pond' online.

What to do:

1. Sing 'Five Little Speckled Frogs' with the children and let them pretend to be the frogs taking turns to jump into the pond.

2. Introduce the word 'amphibians' to the children and explain that these creatures – frogs, toads and newts – can live on land and in water. Explain that recent garden surveys show that the numbers of frogs and toads in the UK are in decline.

3. Talk about the life cycle of the frog using a diagram:

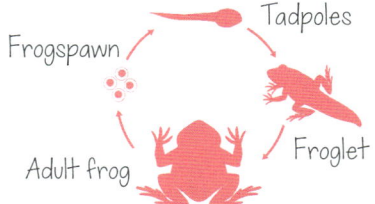

4. Help the children to make life-cycle collages using bubble wrap with black dots for frogspawn, fingerprints with pen tails and limbs for tadpoles and froglets, and green paper circles, googly eyes and concertina legs for the adult frog.

5. Take the children on a trip to a local pond during the months of February and March to find frogspawn or tadpoles. If you find some, make regular trips to observe the frogs going through the three stages of metamorphosis (transformation) from frogspawn to tadpole to frog.

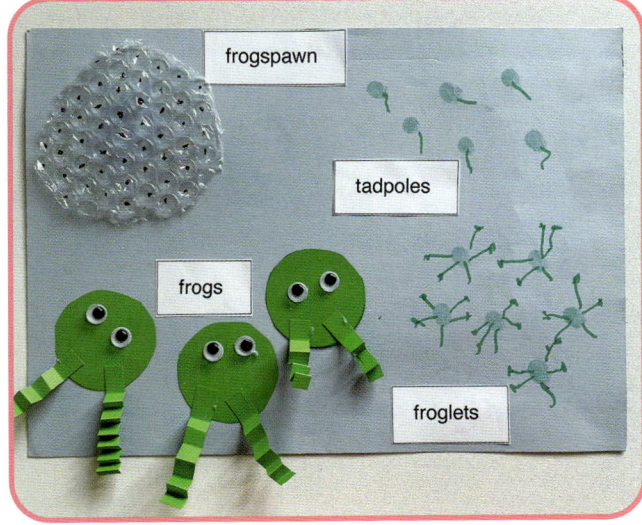

Hosting hedgehogs

Make a hedgehog haven in your outdoor space

What you need:

- Books about hedgehogs, such as *How Can I Help Roly the Hedgehog?* by Frances Rodgers
- A sharp knife or cutting tool or a spade
- A ruler
- A small plastic box
- A plastic tube approximately 13 cm in diameter
- Scissors
- Dry leaves or straw
- Logs or rocks
- Two shallow dishes
- A small tin of cat food and some water

What to do:

1. Share the picture book *How Can I Help Roly the Hedgehog?* or any other books and information about these increasingly rare, nocturnal creatures.

2. Explain to the children that they are going to help hedgehogs join the 'hedgehog highway' by providing an access hole for hedgehogs at the bottom of a fence or hedge.

3. Choose a suitable outside area near to a fence or hedge. Cut or dig out a hole, 13 cm by 13 cm, just big enough for a hedgehog to crawl through. Seek permission from the site supervisor before doing this.

4. Using the tube as a template, cut a hole in one side of the plastic box. Help the children to insert the tube into the hole to create a tunnel.

5. Place the box near to a hedge or fence and help the children to make a cosy nest inside. Cover the box with leaves, twigs and rocks and let the children half fill it with dry leaves or straw.

6. Explain to the children that hedgehogs may choose to hibernate in the nest and will be very hungry and thirsty when they wake. Leave shallow dishes of water and cat food nearby for them to try.

What's in it for the children?

Children will become more aware of how some animals are endangered and need our help to survive.

Taking it forward

- If you are fortunate to see a hedgehog go to www.bighedgehogmap.org to log your hog.

 Health & Safety

Remind the children to wash their hands after handling soil and leaves.

Bees knees

Ideas to save the workers

What you need:

- Paper
- Pencils
- Chalks
- Cotton wool balls
- Outside garden area
- Flowers and plants, such as snowdrops, winter acronite and lavender
- Plant pots
- Windowsill planter or hanging basket (optional)
- Herb seeds or plants, such as mint, thyme and sage (optional)

What's in it for the children?

Children will begin to understand how important bees are to us and how we can help save them by growing a variety of flowers and plants.

Taking it forward

- Find out more about planting a wildflower garden (see page 62), which will help bees to survive.

Health & Safety

Remind the children to wash their hands after handling soil or plants in the garden.

What to do:

1. Talk to the children about the vital job that bees do pollinating plants to provide food for us. Explain how bees feed on sweet nectar, which they then turn into honey. Talk to the children about the reasons that bees are endangered, such as climate change and pesticides that are used on crops.

2. Help the children to understand the process of pollination. Ask each child to draw a picture of a flower on a piece of paper and colour in the middle of the flower using chalk. Choose children to take turns going from picture to picture holding a cotton wool ball to represent a bee visiting each flower. Support them to rub the chalk centre of a flower, and then to fly away to the next one. The children will see how the coloured chalk has transferred from the flower to the bee.

3. Explain to the children that the best way to care for the bees is to improve their habitat. Plant a bee garden with the children containing varieties of plants that flower in every season. Go to friendsoftheearth.uk for lists of suitable shrubs, flowers and herbs and more ideas to attract bees.

4. If you don't have access to a garden, let the children help plant out a windowsill planter or hanging basket with herbs such as mint, thyme and sage.

Wildlife Wednesdays
Timetable your wild activities

What you need:
- An outside space
- Access to online resources

Top tip

Go to worcswildlifetrust.co.uk and find out about becoming wildlife investigators. Help the children to discover the world on their doorstep, whether they are interested in bees, birds or bugs.

What's in it for the children?
Children will regularly be involved in activities outside in nature and learn to appreciate the needs of the world around them.

Taking it forward
- Read *Finding Wild* by Megan Wagner Lloyd, a book that helps children discover the beauty of the natural world and realise that 'wild' exists nearer than you think.

- Try reading *Wild Ideas* by Elin Kelsey with the children and find out how good animals are at solving problems.

What to do:
1. The best way to encourage children to be interested in nature and to care for living things is to regularly be 'in nature'. To achieve this you can timetable spending time outside with them.

2. Choose a day of the week to enjoy wild activities, such as Wednesdays (other days are available!). Try one of the activities in this book each week during your Wildlife Wednesday.

3. Open an outdoor classroom and take your learning outside whatever the weather. Ask the children to design a logo or badge to wear to advertise your Wildlife Wednesday activities.

4. Contact different organisations that schedule wild activities for more ideas. The Wildlife Trusts, www.wildlifetrusts.org, have set the UK's biggest annual nature challenge – 'to do one wild thing a day throughout the month of June'. Join in the '30 Days Wild' and encourage the children's families to also get involved.

5. Share the World Wildlife Fund's junior magazine, 'Go Wild!', to help the children to learn about endangered species, the natural world and other environmental issues.

Twitching tricks

Try some birdwatching and nesting activities

What you need:

- Access to a window or outside space
- Photos or pictures of birds
- Binoculars
- Cardboard tubes
- Sticky tape
- Paper and pencils
- Nest-building materials, such as string, old fabric and feathers

What to do:

1. Ask the children to name as many different birds as they can. Most will know robin and blackbird but introduce new names such as sparrow, blue tit, starling, woodpigeon, great tit, goldfinch, magpie and long-tailed tit. These are some of the most common garden birds in the UK.

2. Show the children pictures of as many of these birds as you can using photos online or in non-fiction books. Look out of the window or go on a walk and see if the children can spot any of the birds you have researched. Use binoculars to look closer at the birds.

3. Support the children to make role-play binoculars by taping together two short cardboard tubes. This helps the children to focus on the birds.

4. Watch clips online of birds building nests, singing songs and feeding on different food.

5. In the spring, help the birds build their nests by collecting suitable materials and leaving them outside for the birds to find. Support the children to cut string into 6 cm lengths, tear short strips of old fabric, and gather dried cut grass. Place the materials on the ground for birds to pick up.

What's in it for the children?

Children will find out more about different types of birds and how they live in our world.

Taking it forward

- Collect some helpful birdwatching books, such as *My First Book of Birds* by Zoë Ingram and *RSPB Nature Guides: Birds* by Catherine Brereton and Kate McLelland, for the children to refer to.

- Encourage the children to take part in the Big Garden Birdwatch organised by the RSPB every January.

✚ Health & Safety

Make sure the children don't leave out pieces of string that are too long because the birds can get tangled up.

Beaks, feet and feathers

Take a close-up look at birds

What you need:

- Shallow bowls containing sunflower seeds and raisins
- Chopsticks and tweezers
- Feathers
- Magnifying glasses
- Plastic beakers
- Water
- Paper towels
- Pipettes
- Cooking oil

What to do:

1. Talk to the children about the features of a bird, such as beak, claws, feathers, eyes and so on.

2. Let the children try to use chopsticks and tweezers to pick up seeds or raisins out of shallow bowls, like a bird using its beak. How easy is it?

3. Explain to the children that they are going to find out how birds use their feathers to fly and keep warm. Let the children handle some feathers; using magnifying glasses, invite the children to look at the hollow shafts and explain that it is this that makes the feathers so light.

4. Try an investigation with small groups of children to discover how feathers keep birds dry. Give each child a beaker of water. Ask them to dip their feather into the water and to describe what happens (the water should roll off). Ask the children to dry their feathers with a paper towel.

5. Invite the children to take turns to use a pipette with some cooking oil. Ask them to watch what happens when they add a few drops of cooking oil to the water and then dip the feather in the solution again. How easy is it to dry now? Talk about how important it is to keep the seas and beaches clean, so that birds' feathers don't get contaminated with oil.

Top tip

Invite someone who owns a pet bird to bring it into the setting so that the children can take a closer look.

What's in it for the children?

There are lots of opportunities for the children to develop their fine motor skills when handling tools and feathers. They will also make observations about conservation and birds.

Taking it forward

- Go on a feather hunt in the outside space, garden or local park. Use a stick to move around stones and logs to find hidden feathers. Can the children work together to find out which type of bird the feathers may have belonged to?

- On a snowy day, look outside for bird tracks. If you can't find any prints, make some bird feet out of pipe cleaners and let the children make their own tracks.

➕ **Health & Safety**

Make sure the children wash their hands after handling feathers.

Feed the birds
Caring for birds in winter

What you need:

- 12 cupcake cases
- A skewer
- String cut into 40 cm lengths
- 250 g suet
- 150 g bird seed or dry mix, such as oats, raisins and sunflower seeds
- A large mixing bowl
- A large spoon
- A saucepan or bowl
- A hob or microwave
- A muffin or cupcake tray
- Teaspoons
- A fridge

What to do:

1. Talk to the children about how difficult it can be for birds to find food in the winter. Explain that they are going to make some seed cakes for the birds to eat.

2. Use a skewer to make a hole in the bottom of each paper cupcake case. Give each child a piece of string and support them to thread the string through the hole. Tie a knot in the string on the inside of the cupcake case.

3. Let the children take turns to help mix all the dry ingredients together in a bowl.

4. Melt the suet in a saucepan on a hob or in a bowl in a microwave. Pour it over the dry mix and take turns to stir gently until it all sticks together.

5. Place the cake cases in a muffin or cupcake tray and help the children to pour or spoon some bird cake mixture into each one.

6. Leave to cool and then place in the fridge until set. When the bird cakes have set, remove from the fridge and ask the children to peel off the cupcake cases.

7. Hang the birdfeeders on branches outside.

What's in it for the children?

Working together to make cakes for the birds develops children's empathy. They will also have the opportunity to practise observation skills as they watch and photograph the birds feeding.

Taking it forward

- Encourage the children to sit quietly and patiently and use a camera to take photos of the birds feeding.

✚ Health & Safety

Supervise the children when using the hob or microwave. Keep cakes away from any cats, dogs and, if possible, squirrels! Avoid using peanuts in case of nut allergies.

A parliament of owls

Discover more about owls

What you need:

- *Owl Babies* by Martin Waddell
- Non-fiction books about owls
- An owl pellet (the undigested parts of an owl's food), available to buy online
- Tweezers
- White paper
- Magnifying glasses
- Rubbish bags
- Plastic gloves
- Litter grabbers

Top tip

Adopt an owl or organise a visit to your setting from an owl expert so the children can observe them close up.

What's in it for the children?

Children will find out details about owls, and how they fit into the ecosystem, as well as what we can do to look after them.

Taking it forward

- Try some simple printing activities with the children using cardboard tubes. Cut the tubes in half lengthways and fold a hinge to create the shape of a bird in flight. Let the children design their own 'murmurations' of birds flying all over the paper.

What to do:

1. Share *Owl Babies* with the children and talk about how the owls were scared that their mother wouldn't come back to look after them.

2. Look at pictures of owls in books and online with the children.

3. Talk about what owls like to eat (insects, worms, snails, fish, frogs, mice and voles).

4. Explain to the children that they are going to find out what an owl has been eating by looking at an owl pellet. Pull the pellet apart using tweezers and place the contents on a sheet of white paper. Invite the children to use a magnifying glass to look more closely at any tiny bones.

5. Introduce the word 'parliament' (a group of owls) to the children, and explain that this name is probably used because owls are thought to be wise. Share some other collective nouns with the children such as 'a gaggle of geese', 'a murder of crows' and 'a charm of finches'.

Health & Safety

Make sure the children wash their hands after the activity.

Animal homes

Go on a habitat hunt

What you need:

- An outside space or local park
- Blue, red and green coloured lollipop sticks or lollipop sticks coloured with marker pens

Top tip

Introduce the topic of homes and habitats by reading *Animal Homes* by Libby Walden and *Whose Habitat is That?* by Lucile Piketty.

What's in it for the children?

Children will observe animal homes and will begin to understand what animals need for a safe habitat.

Taking it forward

- Challenge the children to build a nest using natural materials. Go outside and gather suitable building materials such as twigs, dry leaves and grass. Test the strength of the nest by placing a hard-boiled egg inside the structure.

Health & Safety

Carry out a risk assessment and remind children to wash their hands after the activity.

What to do:

1. Introduce the names of some different animals' homes. Who lives in a nest, a den, a drey, a hole, a sty, a burrow or a web? Make a list of all the animals and their homes that the children know already and share with them some new ones.

2. Explain to the children that animals' homes are found in a variety of habitats or areas. They can be sorted into land, air and water. Can the children tell you an animal for each of these areas?

3. Animals choose different environments or habitats to live in based on their needs. What do the children think animals need in their homes? (Food, water, shelter and a safe place to raise their young.)

4. Explain to the children that they are going to go on a 'habitat hunt' looking for places in the local environment where different animals might live, rather than just looking for the animals themselves.

5. Ask the children to place down on the ground blue lollipop sticks when they find water, red lollipop sticks when they find food and green lollipop sticks when they find shelter.

6. Can they find a good habitat for a squirrel, a blackbird, an ant or a frog?

Pond dipping
Investigating pond life

What you need:

- A local pond or an organised pond dip at a nature reserve
- Small fishing nets
- White trays
- White plastic spoons
- Magnifying glasses
- A camera

Top tip ⭐

Make a pond–dipping check list including dragonflies, damselflies, pond skaters, back swimmer, frogspawn, tadpoles, sticklebacks, frogs and newts.

What's in it for the children?

Children can observe creatures living in a pond and be involved in identifying them and finding out about their habitat.

Taking it forward

- Support the children to build a pond in your own setting (see 'Frogs and toads' on page 41 or go to www.rspb.org.uk). Creating a pond in the local environment will increase biodiversity which in turn helps to tackle climate change.

What to do:

1. Visit a local pond or arrange a trip to a nature reserve. Encourage the children to quietly and carefully approach the water. Start by looking around the edge to see if there are any signs of life.

2. Invite the children to stand still and watch for a few moments. What can they see or hear? Remind the children not to make too much noise or they might scare off some shy creatures.

3. Put a small amount of water into each tray ready for the creatures' short stay. Hand them out to the children along with the nets and spoons.

4. Support the children to lower their nets into the water and move them around gently in a figure-of-eight pattern. Help the children to turn their nets inside out on the tray to release any creatures.

5. Show the children how to gently use their spoon to look at individual creatures more closely.

6. When they have finished looking, support the children to lower their trays and nets back into the water, ensuring that all the creatures are returned to the pond.

➕ Health & Safety

Carry out a risk assessment and always make sure there are enough adults present to supervise the children. Remind the children to wash their hands after touching pond water.

Oceans and rockpools

Learning more about our coasts

What you need:

- A beach (optional)
- Collection bags
- Pictures of ocean creatures, such as whales, dolphins, sharks, fish, octopuses, seals, crabs and seahorses
- A selection of seashells, beach stones and driftwood
- Magnifying glasses
- Pencils
- Pieces of cardboard
- Blue paint
- Glue

What's in it for the children?

Children can make close observations of ocean and coastal animals and plants and talk about caring for them.

Taking it forward

- Encourage the children to return to the beach with their families and carry out a litter pick to help keep the beach clean.
- Talk to the children about how important it is to try to keep the ocean clear of litter and pollution. Read *Somebody Swallowed Stanley* by Sarah Roberts to introduce the topic of pollution in the sea.

Health & Safety

Carry out a risk assessment if visiting a beach and remind the children to wash their hands after handling found items.

What to do:

1. If you are lucky enough to live near to the coast, organise a beach walk. Invite parents and carers to join you and encourage the children to collect items of interest. If you are not able to visit a beach, share pictures of ocean creatures with the children.

2. If the beach has rockpools, let the children explore them to find out about coastal habitats. Invite them to look for inhabitants such as limpets, starfish, crabs and different seaweeds. Ask the children to sit quietly and carefully and watch for life in the pools.

3. Invite the children to collect a few items from the beach, such as seashells, seaweed, pebbles and driftwood.

4. Take the results of the beachcombing back to your setting to sort or, alternatively, have a selection of beach items ready for the children to handle and sort.

5. Provide the children with lots of different shells to touch, smell and examine closely with a magnifying glass. Talk about the different shapes, colours and textures and support the children to make sketches of the shells.

6. Use the beach finds to create some coastal collages. Support the children to create water effects on the cardboard using the blue paint. When dry, encourage the children to stick the shells, seaweed, driftwood and pebbles onto the cardboard.

Underground, overground
Discovering different places to learn, live and grow

What you need:

- A tuff tray
- Sand
- Compost
- Small world animals that live underground, such as rabbits, badgers, foxes and moles
- Cardboard or plastic tubes
- Fiction books about animals and trees, such as *The Tree* by Neal Layton, *The Wild Woods* by Simon James or *How Many Trees?* by Stephanie Barroux

What's in it for the children?

Children can use their fine motor movements to tunnel and burrow into the sand and gross motor movements to walk outside and explore the woods.

Taking it forward

- Provide some root vegetables that grow underground such as carrots, parsnips, swede, turnips and potatoes for the children to handle, draw and wash in the water tray.

Health & Safety
Remind the children to wash their hands after touching the compost.

What to do:

1. Talk to the children about animals that live underground in holes and burrows, such as rabbits, badgers, foxes and moles.

2. Set up an underground habitat in a tuff tray with a mix of sand and compost. Add some small world animals.

3. Ask the children to make holes and tunnels using their hands or the toy animals. How well can the animals hide underground?

4. Provide lots of cardboard or plastic tubes and other resources for the children to use in their tunnelling.

5. Talk to the children about animals that live above ground in trees, such as squirrels, owls and spiders. Read a fiction book about trees and animals and talk about all the different creatures that live in or around trees.

6. Go on a walk to a nearby park, wood or forest and let the children spot different trees and their inhabitants.

7. Play a game of 'Changing Trees' based on Musical Chairs. Each child sits on a chair that represents a tree, and they are a woodland creature. When the music stops, remove one or more chairs and see if the children can still find a tree to live in.

Little collectors

Saving the environment little by little

What you need:

- *A Planet Full of Plastic* by Neal Layton
- A rubbish bag or litter bin
- Plastic gloves
- Litter grabbers
- Card for making posters
- Paints and paintbrushes
- Pencils and felt-tip pens
- Used plastic bottles (washed and dried)
- Scissors
- Bird seed
- Wire or string

What to do:

1. Read *A Planet Full of Plastic* to the children and talk about how much damage litter and the overuse of single-use plastic has done to the earth.

2. Explain that you are going to care for your setting by going on a litter collection.

3. Provide the children with plastic gloves and litter grabbers. Ask them to pick up any litter they spot and place it in the rubbish bag or litter bin as they go.

4. When all the litter has been collected, invite the children to work in groups to design and create some anti-litter posters. Model a poster for the children so that they know the sorts of details to include.

5. Talk to the children about the ways to reuse plastic bottles, such as making a bird feeder.

6. Help the children to use scissors to cut a small oval hole near the top of one side of their bottle so that the birds can get at the seeds. Make a few small holes in the bottom of the bottle for rain to run off.

7. Support the children to fill their bottles with bird seed and attach wire or string around the lid.

8. Hang the bird feeders outside near a window so that the children can watch birds feeding.

Top tip ⭐

Talk to the children about Elizabeth Gadsdon who, at the age of seven, started the Little Collector Crew, a group of children who aim to help to protect the environment from litter and show the places they love some TLC.

What's in it for the children?

Children will become more aware of the changes in the world around them and what they can do to make a difference for the future.

Taking it forward

- Talk about what else the children can do to make a difference to the environment, such as encourage parents and carers to buy loose fruit and vegetables, visit a 'zero waste' shop, use reusable water bottles or increase recycling.

 Health & Safety

Carry out a risk assessment for the litter collection. Remind the children not to pick up hazardous materials such as broken glass or animal poo, and if they are not sure, to check with a grown up. Always ensure that the children wash their hands after litter picking.

Hot and cold
Compare and contrast habitats

What you need:

- Photos of hot and cold habitats
- A sand tray
- Small world animals that live in hot climates, such as snakes, lizards, scorpions, meerkats and camels
- A water tray
- Blocks of ice or ice cubes
- Small world animals that live in cold climates, such as polar bears, seals and penguins
- *Over and Under the Snow* by Kate Messner
- *Fennec Fox or Arctic Fox* by Marilyn Easton

What to do:

1. Show the children photos of two different types of habitat, such as a hot desert and a cold iceberg.

2. Set up a hot desert play area in the sand tray with small world animals, such as plastic snakes, meerkats, scorpions and camels. Talk to the children about how the different animals adapt to live in the hot habitat.

3. Set up a contrasting cold area in the water tray, with floating lumps of ice, using small world animals such as polar bears and seals. Talk to the children about how the different animals adapt to live in the cold habitat.

4. Read *Over and Under the Snow* to the children and find out about the secret world of snow hares, bears and bullfrogs who make their winter homes just under the snow.

5. Explain to the children that some animals have the same name but live in contrasting habitats. Read *Fennec Fox or Arctic Fox* to the children. Invite them to discover how the two foxes survive in the different environments. Extend the discussion by talking about British red foxes and their habitat. Can the children act out how the different foxes might live and adapt?

What's in it for the children?

Children will understand the similarities and differences between two contrasting habitats and the animals that live in them.

Taking it forward

- Add to the desert play area by planting some succulents in an old sand tray or planter.

Acorn to oak
Planting trees to save the planet

What you need:

- *The Extraordinary Gardener* by Sam Boughton
- Access to trees
- Acorns
- Small plastic plant pots
- Peat-free compost
- Sand
- Leaves

Top tip

Share *The Lost Words* by Robert Macfarlane and Jackie Morris with the children and rediscover lots of nature words that will otherwise be lost forever, such as acorn, conker, bluebell and dandelion.

What's in it for the children?

Children will observe trees in their local environment and find out about the life cycle of plants by growing seeds.

Taking it forward

- Try some leaf printing with the children. Invite them to paint the underside of the leaves and then turn them over, pressing gently onto paper and peeling off.

 Health & Safety

Remind the children to wash their hands after handling soil.

What to do:

1. During the autumn, read *The Extraordinary Gardener* with the children.

2. Take the children on a 'tree walk' in your local park, woodland or arboretum. Collect ripe acorns, brown not green, for the children to use to grow an oak tree.

3. Explain to the children that they are going to plant an acorn and grow an oak tree, but that they will have to wait a long time, just like Joe in the story.

4. Support the children to fill the plant pots with some damp peat-free compost mixed with sand. Explain that each plant pot will contain one acorn.

5. Show the children how to push the acorn down into the compost so that it is well covered, keeping the pointed end pointing upwards.

6. Place the pots in a cool place such as a shed or an unheated room so it's not too warm as this will prevent germination. They will not need to be watered during the winter.

7. In the spring, let the children check the pots carefully to see if any of the acorns have sprouted. Water the tiny seedlings regularly and when they are about 25 cm high transfer them into larger pots.

Mini greenhouse
Growing plants indoors

What you need:

- Seeds for herbs, such as basil, chives, dill, mint and parsley
- Seeds for flowers, such as nasturtiums, morning glory, marigolds and viola
- Lollipop sticks
- Felt-tip pens
- A cardboard egg box or seedling tray
- Compost
- Water
- A clear plastic tray to use as a cover (optional)

What to do:

1. Explain to the children that they are going to grow some plants indoors so they can keep a careful watch on them.

2. Look at the different seeds available for herbs and flowers and let the children choose the plants they prefer. Support the children to write their names and the types of plant on lollipop sticks, which will be used to label each pot.

3. Set up the mini greenhouse by filling a cardboard egg box or seedling tray with moist compost. Invite the children to sprinkle a few of their chosen seeds into each pot and to add their lollipop stick label.

4. Cover with a clear plastic tray if available and place in a sunny spot in the setting, such as on a windowsill.

5. Support the children to water the seeds regularly.

6. Take photos of the growing plants at different stages of growth and make a display. Look at the different parts of the plants with the children, such as roots, stems, leaves and flowers.

Top tip

Creating an indoor garden will help avoid the bitter experience of watching young plants being devoured by slugs outside!

50 fantastic ideas for caring for living things

What's in it for the children?

Children will observe change as the seeds germinate and grow into different plants and flowers. There are opportunities for fine motor control when the children plant the seeds.

Taking it forward

- Pick a green leaf from a plant and place it in a bowl of lukewarm water, with a small pebble on top. Place the bowl in a sunny spot for a few hours. Can the children see small bubbles forming around the leaf and edges of the bowl? Explain that the leaf is using the sunlight to create energy (photosynthesis) and then breathing out gas (oxygen) to make bubbles.

➕ Health & Safety

Remind the children to wash their hands after handling soil and seeds.

Beans means...

Start growing your own vegetables

What you need:

- Broad bean seeds
- Wet paper towels
- Glass jars
- Damp cotton wool or paper towels
- Water
- Paper booklets/diaries
- Pencils and felt-tip pens
- A camera

What to do:

1. Show the children a broad bean pod and sing this new version of '5 Fat Peas':

   5 broad beans in a furry pod pressed,
   One grew, two grew, and so did all the rest.
   They grew and they grew, and they did not stop.
   Until one day the pod went POP!

2. Talk to the children about how to wake the bean up so that it will start to germinate (grow). What do the children think it will need to germinate? (Water and sunlight.)

3. Give each child a broad bean seed and ask them to wrap them up in a wet paper towel. Leave them for one hour in a tray to soak up the water.

4. After one hour, help the children to put some damp cotton wool or a cylinder of damp paper towel into a glass jar. Place the bean between the glass and the cotton wool or paper towel. This allows the children to watch the bean split as it starts to grow roots and then shoots.

5. Place all the jars on a windowsill in the sunlight. Remind the children that they will need to water the plants regularly.

6. Ask the children to keep a simple diary of the changes to their bean using drawings and/or photographs. Talk to the children about the names of the different parts of the plant. Can they add labels to their pictures?

What's in it for the children?

Children observe close up the changes that take place as a plant grows and gain an understanding of the different parts of plants and the life cycle that plants go through.

Taking it forward

- Try growing some other vegetables with the children for them to eat.

 Health & Safety

Remind the children to wash their hands after handling soil and seeds.

Water watch

Learning about the importance of water

What you need:

- A 2 L clear plastic bottle
- A permanent marker
- A ruler
- A bottle of food colouring
- Water
- A small bowl
- A clear glass jar
- Shaving foam
- A dropper or pipette

What's in it for the children?

Children learn about the importance of water to our health and safety in the world. They will observe different weather conditions and record the changes that they see.

Taking it forward

- Make a weekly weather chart and invite the children to record the weather each day. Invite them to make different weather symbols for sun, rain, cloud, rainbow, snow, wind and so on.

What to do:

1. Explain to the children that all plants and animals need water and rain is an important source of water. Tell them that they are going to make a rain gauge.

2. Cut the top off a 2 L plastic bottle, turn it upside down and place it inside the main body of the bottle.

3. Using the ruler and a permanent marker, help the children to measure 5 cm, 10 cm, 15 cm and 20 cm lines up the side of the bottle. Place the rain gauge outside and invite the children to take turns to record the daily rainfall.

4. Explain to the children that they are going to do an experiment to make it rain inside.

5. Support the children to mix a few drops of food colouring with a little bit of water in a small bowl.

6. Fill a clear glass jar about a third full with clear water. Squirt shaving foam on the top of the jar to make a fluffy cloud.

7. Using the dropper to suck up some coloured water from the bowl, ask the children to take turns to squirt it onto the cloud until it rains.

Wildflower garden
Try some rewilding in your setting

What you need:

- Wildflower seeds, such as meadow buttercup, St John's wort, poppies, lady's bedstraw, birdsfoot trefoil, chamomile, corn marigolds and cornflowers

- Empty food cylinders with plastic lids

- Seed catalogues and garden magazines

- Scissors

- PVA glue

- Paintbrushes

- Bradawl or knitting needle

- Sticky tape

- A suitable outdoor space or windowsill planter

- A rake

What to do:

1. Explain to the children that they are going to plant a wildflower garden to help bees and butterflies.

2. Show the children the packets of wildflower seeds and let them compare the different shapes and sizes of the seeds.

3. Support the children to make their own seed shakers. Let them cut out pictures of flowers and plants from seed catalogues and garden magazines.

4. Invite the children to glue the pictures around the outside of an empty food cylinder.

5. Under adult supervision, ask the children to make several holes in the plastic lid using a bradawl or knitting needle. The holes need to be big enough for the seeds to flow through easily.

6. Invite the children to place some seeds in their shakers. Secure the lids of the shakers with sticky tape.

7. If your setting has a suitable outdoor space, go outside and show the children how to rake the soil in the flower bed ready for the seeds. Ask them to gently shake the seeds onto the soil. Alternatively a windowsill planter can be used.

Top tip ⭐

Go to www.beebombs.com and find out about beebombs, or www.woodlandtrust.org.uk to buy native wildflower seedballs, that can help to create a wildflower meadow and in turn help bees and butterflies to thrive.

What's in it for the children?

Children can use a variety of tools to make seed shakers and plant out a wildflower garden to help insects in the environment.

Taking it forward

- Set up a nectar café as part of your wildflower garden with flowering plants to attract butterflies, moths and bees. Remember to leave areas of the garden untidy to provide places for insects to thrive.

- Talk to the children about what else is living in the soil and find out more in *Up in the Garden and Down in the Dirt* by Kate Messner.

- Open a garden centre in the role-play corner with packets of flower and vegetable seeds, pots, plants, garden tools, wellington boots and so on.

✚ Health & Safety

Remind the children to wash their hands after handling soil and seeds.

Guess who?

Looking at the past and the future

What you need:

- *Here We Are: Notes for Living on Planet Earth* by Oliver Jeffers
- Photos of children and staff as babies
- Photos of baby animals or pets
- Paper
- Paints and paintbrushes
- A soft toy

Top tip

Start a 'Be Kind Jar' with strips of paper inside suggesting things that the children can do for each other.

What's in it for the children?

Children can see similarities and differences between themselves and others and can begin to understand how the past affects the present and the future.

Taking it forward

- To remind the children about caring for each other, let children make some 'Be Kind' badges to wear and to give to others. Use circles of cardboard and ask them to draw a speech bubble on each one with the words 'Be Kind' inside.

What to do:

1. Explain to the children that we have been learning about caring for and about living things. We are all living things too and an essential part of the ecosystems on planet Earth.

2. Read *Here We Are: Notes for Living on Planet Earth* to the children. Discuss how important it is to be kind to each other, to all living things, and to the earth.

3. Invite the children and practitioners in the setting to bring in a photo of themselves as a baby. Include some pictures of baby animals or pets for the children to identify.

4. Display the pictures on a board and invite the children to try to recognise each other. How much or how little have they changed?

5. What do the children think they will look like when they grow up even more?

6. Invite them to paint portraits or triptychs (an artwork in three parts) of themselves as a baby, now and in the future.

7. Encourage the children to talk about their dreams for the future and what they might like to do. Sit in a circle and pass around a soft toy inviting the children to share their dreams and hopes with each other.